MAN
UP-LIFTING

A New Standard For
LOVE, LEADERSHIP & LOYALTY

ALFRED DUNCAN.
WITH VICTORIOUS HALL

DEDICATION

This book is dedicated to Blake (my son) and Chauncey (my nephew). You two have inspired me to challenge myself and the concept of manhood as I knew it to be when I was your age. This book is also dedicated to my mother Sheila Duncan, sister Tonya Duncan and my niece Tiyawna Duncan. My entire outlook on life has been molded by the love that you have provided me with.

- Alfred

To my wife,
The man I am is directly correlated to the woman you are.
Thank you for always seeing the best in me.

– Victorious

CONTENTS

PART 1:
LOVE

MAN UP-LIFTING

CHAPTER I.

PHYSICAL

⬅——————————————————➡

Taking care of yourself is taking care of God...
- Alfred "Black" Duncan

Let's be honest men. We are not the greatest when it comes to taking care of our physical selves. I'm not necessarily talking about the six pack abs and the guns/biceps either, although they are a part of our physical frames. Let's talk about "care" like staying up on your regular doctor visits or being proactive about scheduling an appointment when you have been having chest pains for two months. Let's talk about that athlete's foot that you keep powdering to death to cover up the smell. Let's talk about getting your prostate checked and having a colonoscopy. Yeah, I saved the "colonoscopy" for last, because I know some of you cringed and probably said "pause" or "no homo" when you read that. **I'm sure if there were a "manhood handbook," getting a colonoscopy would not make it pass the first draft,** because to most of us, it's "unmanly" to allow anything in your anus - even if it could save your life. I feel you brother. It makes me cringe too, however if a colonoscopy has the potential to increase my lifespan and award me the opportunity to spend more time with the ones I love, then I just need to "Man Up."

It's time for a tune-up...

- Black

I'm not a big alcohol drinker, and my co-author and best man Vic is not a drinker at all. He has never had one sip of alcohol in his life, and that's pretty amazing to me… Enough about him; I think he'll tell you more than enough in the pages that follow. **So I've always been told that I shouldn't mix light and dark liquors or I would get sick.** I don't necessarily believe this theory, but I've heard it so much that I follow that rule, because it just may be right. I know people who swear by this rule. I also know people who are more sophisticated with their drinking rules. I have one friend who says that he doesn't drink dark liquor because it makes him violent. I have another friend who says that he drinks a beer in the morning to get rid of a hangover from the night before.

It's amazing how in tune a man can be with his body when the consequences are immediate. If only we could use that power for good. What if you really listened to your body about everything? What if you knew when your body needed exercise, sleep, water, fruit, etc.? What if you were so in tune with your body that it warns you that you are about to get sick, which would cause you to take preventive measures to lessen the effects of a looming illness? That would be dope right? What if you were so in-tune with your body that it helped you make very important decisions...the go with your gut type of decisions? Well this is attainable. And you attain it by listening to your body. I mean deep listening, similar to "listening" to Young Thug's album and writing down all of his lyrics word for word. Yup, that type listening… that thorough. It's a lot of work but that's what manhood is about.

*Manhood is about stepping up and being
"in tune."*
- Victorious "VIC" Hall

Do you really think that we like the taste of Mc-
Donald's? Our physical bodies can't really like McDonald's. Some people indulge in eating from this restaurant
several times a day, as if it is gourmet food. But once you
become in tune with yourself, you begin to realize that it is
just a huge marketing campaign. We don't really enjoy the
food. We may enjoy the food temporarily, but the long-term
and often immediate effects of the grease, artificial ingre-
dients and toxins make many of us sick. We don't like the
way our body feels after eating it. But, it's convenient and
marketed very well. Tuning in or being in tune doesn't
mean that we stop eating foods that are no good for us all
the time, but it does mean that we begin to become aware
of how the things that we put in our bodies affect our out-
put. It means that we consider when and how much "good
stuff" and "bad stuff" we put into our bodies. **Being in tune
means that we understand how our actions influence
everyone else around us.** When we treat our bodies well,
the people around us begin to feel compelled to do the
same. Staying in tune means that we are aware of how
everything – be it food, environment, or attitude – are
impacting the quality of our lives on a daily basis. We are

mindful of the decisions we make each day and how they contribute to our overall well-being and success. We are aware of what we are putting into our bodies, minds and spirits. We are in tune of what our bodies may need to be at optimal performance.

Most of us can easily tell when our bodies are hungry. Signals begin to fire up in our brains, letting us know that it is time to eat. However, most of us have a difficult time knowing what our body truly needs to sustain and perform at our greatest. So we instead we choose to eat the most available or best marketed food options.

Staying in tune simply means that we should live lives of balance to ensure that we are enjoying life. It also means that we are considerate and thankful to the creator for giving us the opportunity to live. So it's alright to know which meal a #3 is from McDonald's, but we should also know what daily vitamins and minerals our bodies need. We can choose to drink alcohol on certain days of the week, but it also means we should intake green vegetables daily and drink water consistently to ensure all of our systems and organs are functioning properly.

I am of the belief that when we start to become aware of how we choose to operate in our daily lives, then our choices start to become more consistent and our lives begin to improve. **Love for self begins with an examination of our daily practices**.

You shouldn't look better than your wife...
-Black

When I was growing up, my generation wasn't really into the "metro sexual" thing, per se. However, the times have changed, and a lot of men are into their appearance just as much as women are. I have no problem with that. I can't encourage you to love yourself and then turn around and bash you for wanting to present your best appearance to the world. Go for it homie. However, the woman was designed to be a work of art amongst other things. Please know that the woman is really the show. You are just the supporting cast. Yeah, I know it may be hard to swallow, considering we are in a world where a lot of men are self-absorbed and they work hard to become a commodity, so they can have options in women. It's hard to tell a man to build himself up and then find a wife and take a backseat. When put that way, not many men will sign up for that. Especially an insecure one who seeks the spotlight just as much as his counterpart. **But trust me: if you find a SUITABLE wife/girlfriend that compliments you and you lift her up, you will ultimately be lifting yourself up**. I am an example of this. I wanted to honor my then girlfriend Sherrell with a special day that would blow her mind. I wanted to make her feel like the greatest woman in the world, and so I figured I'd plan an engagement and then surprise wedding just six hours later, on the same day. *What I did* was all about honoring HER and showing HER how much I love HER. Myself and everyone involved created and executed #ForeverDuncan with nothing but love. Look what happened. It launched us into the spotlight and put us on a platform to do things like write books. Although I was the visionary behind #ForeverDuncan, the end result had nothing to do with me. It was all about my wife. People fell in love with her response, her life prior to this, her praise, her feelings. People *just* wanted to know how I pulled it off, but they wanted to know *everything* about my wife. I am rarely noticed when I walk out of my home alone.

However, if I go anywhere with my wife, people often approach us for pictures, conversation and even autographs. All of the attention is on my wife. She can't go anywhere without someone noticing her and requesting a picture. I'm so cool with that though. I know she is the show, and I'm cool with supporting her throughout the production. I think that's what manhood is all about. You can be a doctor married to a stay-at-home mother. Your money may fund the project, but please know that she is the show. She keeps things flowing. She keeps things in order. She is the biggest facilitator and the biggest threat to your happiness.

Our outer appearance plays a major part in how we love our physical selves...
- VIC

As men, however, we should not attempt to prove ourselves through our clothes. It's foolish and childish to adorn yourself in high fashion to prove your worth or your status to those around you. In real life, who cares about the brand name of your clothes, besides (of course) other people who share those same inferiority issues? Manhood is less about being flashy and more about being humble. As men, we should be spending a considerable amount of time working on our internal appearance. **Our internal intelligence, confidence and sustainability are what makes us appealing to everyone else.**

Now with all that said, I firmly believe in style. I think style is something that we have possessed for a long time. Our individual style separates each person from the pack. It influences our moves and actions. It dictates how the world views us. And it speaks for us before we part our lips. Our style helps to manage and encourage our interactions.

My son, who is 8, is clearly developing his own style. As a father, you naturally want your child to emulate much of what and how you interact with the world stylistically, but my son is clearly developing his own way. Initially, I had father shock. I experienced moments of unfamiliarity when I watched him get dressed and then step out into the world. Then I began to realize how his style influences his interactions with the world. I began to think about where he was deciding to place his value and how that impacts how he interacts with the world. I realized that his style works for him. It's not my job to try to change it, because I want him to look or act a certain way. I should be more like a guide, facilitating his awesomeness. Which in short, this is what I think our style should do. It should expose our awesomeness. And our awesomeness is not dictated by looking better than anyone else, outshining our partners, driving the most expensive cars, wearing the most expensive shoes or wearing chains and earrings that attract people's attention. Instead, our style should be a reflection of what's happening with us internally.

CHAPTER II.

SPIRITUAL

←——————————————————————————→

Take into account that you are connected to something greater than yourself...
- VIC

Many try to emulate "spirituality" with religious standards and norms, but the truth is that few people know what "spirituality" truly means. All we know truly is that whoever created us is a bad mopo! Because of this, it is important that we know that self-care is God care. We are ultimately just vessels of the most high, trying to figure ourselves out to ensure we are doing the right work. When we take care of ourselves, we are taking care of God. God's presence lives through our existence. The true nature of God cannot be realized without a conceptual understanding from people. Therefore, it is important that we keep that at the forefront of our minds when we are chosen to love God in other forms. In short, God is a manifestation. And to truly appreciate the God in others, we must first begin to understand how God moves through us. **There is**

no way to truly identify the supreme spirit in our significant others or our children if we cannot first recognize this spirit within ourselves.

We are all plugged into the same outlet. Our source of energy is God. God, by definition is supreme energy. That supreme energy is manifested through our daily interactions, and it is essential that we consistently keep that in mind as we navigate through the world everyday. We were all born to be awesome, everyone!

There are two things that I dislike: 1. folks who think they are better than others. 2. folks who have trouble celebrating another man's awesomeness. To be humble is a part of manhood. Humility does not mean that you are down playing yourself, but rather you are able to recognize and support the greatness in others you may interact with. Let's take my friendship with Black, for example. We are both clearly awesome at different things. So I'm awesome at being fly, smart, funny, a toddler and elder's go-to guy… plus I can chef up a mean spaghetti. I think Black is pretty good at music. (See what I did there?) Should I downplay his musical abilities just because I am a handsome, charismatic chef, who is well-respected among toddlers and elders? In all seriousness, when you're humble, you are not in competition with anyone. Instead you are in constant reflection with yourself and you have respect for the journey of others. The ability to see God's presence in others is the baseline for spiritual grounding and development. It is also the foundation of humility. It is the ability to know that God's energy is inside of you, but simultaneously understanding that the same energy that makes you amazing is inside of every soul and physical feature that you interact with daily. Humility is the ability to truly feel God's presence. Being aware of God's presence helps to keep us aligned and in tune.

Everybody is a self-proclaimed "Boss" in this day and age. Even though most clearly work a 40-hour work week to make someone else's dream come true...
- Black

Webster states that a "boss" is a person who exercises control or authority; *specifically*: one who directs or supervises workers. *The Urban Dictionary* states that a boss is a person who is a leader, someone who runs shit in his/her hood or city. I love when my people urbanize a word, but I'm not a big fan of the word "boss." I think it promotes divisiveness and selfishness. I think the so-called "boss" mentality makes people focus solely on their personal objectives and not the collective plight of our communities. Prior to "boss" being glorified by rappers, we didn't necessarily like bosses. Bosses were considered to be inconsiderate and insensitive tyrants, jerks, sometimes incompetent and unworthy of the positions in which they held... oh and they were typically thought to be disrespectful. Terrible bosses only bring people together because employees share the same disdain for the person in leadership. Bosses, whether good or bad, are the primary reason that employees either love or hate their jobs.

I have a different outlook on being a "boss." I think a boss should be more like a concierge than an overseer. A great boss has a keen eye for great talent and creates an atmosphere that helps nurture that talent to be the best it can possibly be. A great boss motivates his/her team by inspiring them versus threatening them. A great boss has invested interest in the future of his/her employees. A great boss recognizes and rewards great work. A great boss builds up his/her employees, and, in return, employees work hard to build up his/her company. A great boss loves to lead from the front and show his employees that he/she is willing to endure whatever is expected from employees. A great boss is someone who knows that it's not all about them. As a matter of fact, it's not about them at all. It's about the task at hand. Manhood is similar to this great boss idea. Manhood isn't glamourous. Manhood rarely comes with recognition. With manhood comes difficult decisions that you must make for the better of the collective.

Understand and live in your greatness, but always remain humble...

- Black

I have accomplished some amazing feats in my life-time. However, I have a hard time talking about them without inquiry. I do not like promoting myself or listing my accomplishments, because it feels like I am being arrogant or conceited. I feel very awkward talking about myself. If someone sees my accomplishments as something that needs to be praised or pointed out, then that's on them. The corniest guy to me is that one dude who has little fame to his name, but pulls the "You don't know who I am?" card when he can't get into the club. I figure if you don't know who I am, then I guess I have to work harder to make you know at a later date. I don't do what I do to be acknowledged. I work because I am passionate about my art. I will admit, it feels great to be recognized for your work, but I want it to be organic, not processed.

My wife and friends tell me that I am too modest. I would rather say that I am humble, but I try my best to shy away from self-proclaimed titles. In my mind, the moment I say that I am humble, I am being arrogant. The moment I say that I am a professional, I am being unprofessional. The moment I say that I am famous, I am being typical. I believe that the Lord has blessed me to be great in many

17

areas. However, most talents that I have been blessed with are judged with a subjective scope. So it's not for me to say that I am great at anything. My work should speak to those who think that I'm great. I don't like to talk about greatness. I prefer to walk in greatness. I want my actions to speak louder than my words. Unfortunately, we live in a world where words garner success more than work. If you have the right promotion and marketing strategy, you can make garbage look like the best thing since sliced bread. This route is often short-lived because, despite popular belief, consumers aren't dumb. They catch on eventually. I've done some major things that I haven't been recognized for, but instead of bitching and complaining, I just kept producing and executing my ideas. Funny how a production that I put together just to show my wife how much I love her has given me a platform that I had been seeking for years.

I had no idea #ForeverDuncan would turn into this. God has blessed me for being committed to walking in my greatness without worrying about the recognition. I won't lie to you and act like it didn't bother me that my work was going unnoticed, but that's life. That's also manhood. Manhood is about doing the work to the best of your ability without focusing on the recognition that comes with it. The recognition will come. It may not come when you think it should. It may not come the way you think it should, but it will come. Michael Jordan is arguably the best basketball player to ever play the game. When asked, "Who was the toughest defensive player you ever played against?" He replied Joe Dumars. For the youngins' reading this book, who may not know who Joe Dumars is, he was a shooting guard for the Detroit Pistons from 1985 to 1999. He was a beast. I always loved Joe's game, because he was so quiet, but he would burn you up at any given time. Joe Dumars may not get the praise and/or recognition that Michael Jordan gets, but he did get praise and recognition from Michael Jordan himself. The praise will come and go, but the work is permanent. Man-Up and don't talk about your greatness, just walk in your greatness.

MAN UP-LIFTING

CHAPTER III.

MENTAL

←——————————————————————————→

Read...

-Black

Growing is a wonderful feeling. To experience growth and recognize it at a later date is one of the best feelings in the world. When I look back at what I use to be, in comparison to what I am now, I can't help but smile. I'm also sure that I will be smiling in the future, when I look back at this moment and see the growth from now to then. As a man, it is very important that you love yourself enough to know that you need to grow mentally and work towards this objective on a daily basis. Renew your mind. No one wants to be the same man they are today on this same date next year. So it's funny how we hold on to the mantra, "I will never change." Change is great. It ultimately means that you have grown and anything that doesn't experience growth anymore is dead. You can obtain this growth in many facets of your life. One practice that I challenge you to take on in order to grow is reading. Reading does not get the credit it deserves. Reading a good book will stimulate you beyond your belief. It increases your vocabulary. It creates better writing skills. It creates a better attention span. Reading can offer encouragement and solutions to your everyday dilemmas. I personally like reading autobiographies, because they tell the entire story about someone who I may admire. These books allow me to see their failures as well as their successes. It shows me a human element of a person beyond what is displayed when the lights and cameras are turned on. Reading is a supreme source of knowledge. You can literally read about anything that interests you. I wasn't a big reader in my younger days, and I can honestly say that I don't currently read as much as I should, but I understand the power of it. I am an on again, off again reader. If I start reading a book that peeks my interest, it is extremely hard to put it down. But once I put it down, it is extremely hard for me to pick it up again. Not because I lost interest, but because I lack discipline in some areas of my life, so I am easily distracted. I am often reminded of the book when I use something that I learned from the book in my everyday life.

This reminder makes me run back to the book to soak up more of its knowledge. One of my goals for the past couple of years was to read at least one book a month. I would pick up a book and start reading it and eventually get bored with it. Since I knew I lacked discipline in finishing books, I would force myself to finish reading the book. This didn't work because I dreaded being bored while reading the book. One day I overheard someone say, "There are too many books in this world to force yourself to read one that you don't enjoy." After hearing this and applying it, it has been extremely easy for me to finish books. So I challenge you to read at least one book a month. It can be about anything that interests you. It will change your life, and that's what you want right? Man-Up and welcome the Change up.

I don't believe that we can fully become men without being well-read…
- VIC

We need to be well-read and well taught. I believe that we need a firm understanding of our legacy in this country. Without connecting your life to the lives of other Black men and women throughout the diaspora, it is essentially impossible to evolve. Our manhood is inter-linked with the men and women that came before us and the men that will follow us when we transition. Just moving through the world as if it's just "us" or "me" without firmly connecting your life to those before you and those after you is to disconnect yourself from our progression. Being well-read means actively engaging oneself in intellectual dis-course as much as possible. It means that you are engaging in conversations that push your understandings of the world. **It means that when you get together with your friends, you are not only discussing the latest football or basketball game, but also discussing freedom, justice and equality for people of color and humanity holisti-cally.**

Expose yourself to new information that is counter to your narrative…
- Black

One thing that I don't like about myself is that I am constantly affected by any kind of negativity that is thrown my way. My wife hates that I get engulfed in finding and viewing the negative just to try to counter it. It actually works for me though. I had a basketball career that lead to two high school championships and a short-lived appearance in a college Division III NCAA tournament. I was naturally good in all sports, but I wasn't serious about any of them. The day I became serious was when a recreation manager saw me practicing in the gym, and he asked me what I was practicing for. I told him that I was trying out for my high school basketball team, and his response was, "You will never make the team." From that point on, I worked tirelessly just to prove him wrong. Negativity works for me, but I dislike that I give so much attention to those who don't support me, when the people who love and support me far outweigh those who don't.

Although I would love to change this aspect of my being, it has taught me a very critical life lesson: it is important to find-listen to-and consider information that counters your beliefs and ideas. I think it either shows you that you have more research to do relating to your belief or it makes you work harder to prove someone or something wrong. I think it becomes hazardous when negativity is our main focus. We have to be open to the counter info, because it can honestly provide a different perspective on our thoughts. It may just change your mind about things.

We are so quick to label something as "hate" if it doesn't agree with our thoughts. But sometimes what we deem as "hate" is constructive and important criticism that can give us a different outlook. I am a firm believer that people constantly clash because we don't practice understanding. Understanding isn't necessarily agreeing with someone, but it's having empathy for their point of view. Understanding is trying your best to see where another person is coming from. Everyone is a product of their upbringing, so each person's opinion has been molded by their experiences over the years. There is no way I can change that, but if I understand what created this opinion, then it makes their opinion easier to swallow. It is healthy to challenge your beliefs, because you are not God. You don't have all the answers sway. Man-Up to the fact that you could be wrong.

Reconnect with the passion for learning you had in your youth...
- VIC

Think back to when you were young. It was probably easy to jump into something new and learn new things, right? We would join a team, visit a new place, and interact with new people very naturally. But somehow as we grew older, things began to change. We are not as interested in allowing ourselves to learn something new and do something different; we seem to become puppets of the socialization that has created us. Preparing ourselves mentally means that we are actively fighting against the systems that try to socialize us to believe ideas and themes that are not true to our historical spiritual selves. **To be a Black man in America means that we are preparing ourselves mentally each day to fight against the oppressive systems that seek to destroy us and our true connections of the world.** Being a Black man in America means being aware that what we are and how we see ourselves are directly interlinked with oppressive systems that have converged upon us. And to be a powerful Black man, we must first begin to think about how our power is constantly taken away daily... How we are taught to not appreciate and love ourselves. How in the world are we led to believe that we are not awesome, magnificent or great? If Black male oppression is foreign to you, it is important that you begin to consider, read and analyze how your worldview and understanding of "self" have been impacted by forces outside of yourself.

Reconnect with the youthful passion you had for learning new things and apply that to exploring the historical context of Black men in the world and country.

Teach yourself new things...
- Black

In my opinion, YouTube is the best teacher in the world. Vic would probably hate that I said that considering the fact that he is a vice principal and an esteemed teacher... but so what. We'll let him be mad. I personally go to YouTube and teach myself any and everything. YouTube has taught me how to use Photoshop, how to break an Amazon Fire TV Stick, how to repair my car, how to clean the built up dirt on the drip pan of my stove, how to replace a part on my television... I could go on and on about the most amazing teacher around—YouTube. I bet YouTube could teach you how to build a house from scratch. If you can't find it on YouTube, then I'm certain you can find it in a book.

I recently had a friend call me and ask me to break his Firestick. He had another buddy who would charge him $75 to break it. Because this is one of my close friends, I chose to do this for him free of charge. Before I agreed to do it, I told him to look on YouTube and do it himself. He didn't want to do it and said that he isn't good at that type of stuff. In this world, there are buyers and sellers. Sellers hold knowledge and skills in particular fields, and they charge people for either giving the knowledge out or using the knowledge to perform a task for the buyer. A buyer doesn't have the knowledge or the skill, so he is paying for the services of someone who does. We are all buyers and sellers at some point in our lives. The key is to make sure you're a seller more than a buyer. In this generation of technology, there is no excuse why you can't be the seller most often. I think manhood is about selling more than buying. I think it is very important for you to add on to your list of skills and abilities on a consistent basis. Sellers inevitably pass down their skills and knowledge to their kids and so they can become sellers too. So learn something new. If not for you, then for your offspring, to whom you will eventually pass down your knowledge. Man-Up and Learn Up all that you can.

CHAPTER IV.

HISTORY

←──────────────────────────────→

How will you help your extended family, who share your origin?

- VIC

Black people are not from South Carolina! Nah, for-real, it's important that we pay homage to our roots here in America, but it is just as important to respect our roots across the Atlantic as well. I know what you're thinking? I ain't from Africa! Hell if you ain't! We all are. The oldest known human bones, the greatest civilizations, and the seat of humanity were all found in the places that we were brought from. In addition, the people who kidnapped us, knew these things, so they had to ensure that we developed a negative image about our home to ensure we didn't connect. So, I agree. You are from South Carolina, but you originated in Africa.

I understand why we choose to associate with the idea that our history begins in America. It's partly because it is difficult to associate with the cultures on the African continent. For many, saying "I am from the south," gives one the ability to connect with an extended family, and it silences the frustrations of not knowing the exact location of our origin. For many, our families are a bi-product of the history that they have endured for hundreds of years. So to properly love our extended families, we have to fully understand the type of love they may need.

Some of our family members may have been through some rough times in their lives, some may be unemployed, looking for housing, or have substance abuse issues, while others may be struggling monetarily. Our job as men is to help take care of our families while making sure we are taking care of ourselves. There is a fine line between providing help, but also ensuring that you are not jeopardizing your own progression. So, when assisting your family, make sure that you are also making sure that you are not putting yourself in a situation that can be a problem.

My wife once told me to always lend things to people with the intent that you will never get it back. This is the best rule of thumb on how to love your extended family. Extend yourself, but don't over extend yourself. We are all here to serve and help one another, but the first law of nature is self-preservation.

To truly love our families means that we have to spend some time to know where we originate from. What is our place of origin? And though your immediate family may play a major part in your understandings of the world, how much do we truly understand about our historical legacy?

For years I had been what you would call "A lost black man…"
- Black

I existed only in the culture that I was born, with no interest of knowing my deeper roots. Vic and I used to host The Up and Up (UAU) Open Mic here in Washington, DC, and we would have African cultural acts perform authentic African music. They would also dress in African garments. Because this was foreign to me, I use to make fun of it. Not because I didn't identify with it fully, but because I thought it was funny and that I would get a good laugh from it. I had no shame in doing this. I would offend many people with my antics at UAU, but I didn't care, because in my opinion, I was an entertaining host and people were laughing. That was my job: to keep people in the building, which meant to keep them entertained. To this day, I have no remorse about jokes that I have made at the expense of others, except the jokes that I made about Africa. When I told these jokes, a part of me was embarrassed, because I was joking about something that I did not know about. So I was coming from an ignorant place. See I think it's cool to make jokes about life. I don't like to be serious all the time. However, if I don't really know about the subject in which I'm joking about, then I'm really criticizing it. Funny enough. I was criticizing a place where I am deeply rooted, so I was un-

33

knowingly criticizing myself. My guilt led me to want to know more about my roots. Not just in Africa, but here in America too. Learning more about your roots is learning more about you. It goes back to my point about understanding. Information promotes understanding. Understanding promotes peace. Inner peace is definitely a key to manhood. Get you some (peace). Man-Up.

I was raised by a beautiful, strong, amazing single woman ...
- Black

My mom's name is Sheila Duncan. My Father wasn't a deadbeat dad, however he wasn't there as much as I would have liked him to be. Another crucial contributor to my growth was my sister Tonya Duncan. I have never in my life seen two women who were so strong in their love, opinions, ideas and faith in God. It was just my mother, sister and I until my sister gave birth to my beautiful niece, Tiyawna Duncan. She was my everything. She would follow me around all the time, and I would use her to get attention from women, because she was "sooooo cute." Up until her birth, my household protected me, but when she was born, I took on the role of the protector... or at least I thought I did.

My family had a way of making me feel that I was protecting them when they were in the back of me intimidating the person in front of me with their hard stares. My core, which is what we called our squad, was such a tight-knit unit. More often than not, on Saturdays we would share the company of each other and playfully converse and debate all day about everything under the sun. My mother created such a safe environment to speak freely about uncomfortable subject matters. My friends would often join in on some Saturday conversations with my family. Some actually came in my house high off weed without knowing that they were about to get pulled into an all-day debate. You would think that they would be blown right? Nah, they actually loved it. They loved the fact that they were accepted into my home despite doing some "hoodlum" stuff, minutes prior to coming into the house. Oh, my mother definitely knew they were high, but she never confronted them about it in a reprimanding way. They loved the fact that they could be so honest with an adult and not be judged. They loved the fact that these two beautiful black women were strong in their opinions, but humble enough to concede to a good point made. I was raised in this environment, so I didn't see what the big deal was. This was normal to me, but my friends would constantly tell me how dope my family was and how "it's not like that" at their homes. At an early age, I began to realize that I was being loved differently than most people in my hood. I wouldn't say "loved more," just loved differently. As an adult, I have a better understanding of the love that I give because I have a better understanding of how I was loved. Having a better understanding of anything gives you an advantage.

Family boundaries are important for personal growth...

- VIC

I remember when I was going through a pretty rough patch in my life. I wanted everyone around me to feel and help me through my pain. I wanted them to share the load, so that I wouldn't have to deal with my own shortcomings. They were placing boundaries on me. The struggle I endured was necessary for my growth.

When you are interacting with your family, there must be clear boundaries that allow you to assist your family members when necessary, but also give space for folks to go through the difficulty of growth through struggle. The aforementioned stance also means the same for us when we seek assistance from our families. We must be mindful of the balance between help and work. Asking for help is oftentimes necessary for survival, but we can't negate the growth attached to the work we must do for ourselves. Without boundaries, people will have the opportunity to take full advantage of everything you have to offer, without the work associated with the blessings.

Love yourself and your extended family. Give and ask for what you can, however, be sure to set clear boundaries for your expectations of yourself and your family. In doing this, everyone can continue to grow and develop into the powerful spirits that we were made to be.

My immediate family tried their best to protect me from harm and disappointments...

- Black

From about age seven throughout my teenage years, my immediate family tried their best to protect me from harm and disappointments. My sister specifically hated when her little brother was let down by something or someone. I was the type of kid that believed what anybody told me. I would get excited if anyone promised me something. Of course I was let down a lot. My family knew this about me, so they tried their best to shield me from this. There is no way that they could prevent all disappointment, and so many disappointments slipped through the cracks.

As I grew older, I learned to accept disappointments without much emotion attached to them. I also learned that I shouldn't trust everyone. My family meant well by trying to protect my heart, but they also did a disservice to my growth. It took me longer to learn that people weren't always honest. It's natural to try your best to keep your loved ones out of harm's way, but we must be cognizant of the experience that we are blocking as well. There are just some things that life has to teach you. No friend, wife or family member can give you the lesson that comes with getting your butt kicked by life. Manhood is definitely about protecting your family, but it's also about having discernment to know when to protect or when to let someone learn on their own.

Ever since the wedding I've been told that I raised the bar too damn high…
- Black

My brothers were pissed at me. Y'all are not really pissed, but I get it. If I was in your shoes, I would've been 'kinda' pissed too. You were over there minding your business, and here I come just busting up in your relationship to make you ask yourself, "Do you really love her?" I would be pissed too if someone me or my girl/wife don't know makes me confirm or reconfirm my love for her, because she is currently feeling some type of way about some random video she saw on Facebook and Instagram. See, she saw a fairytale come true in her mind, so in her mind, you're either her Prince Charming or you're not, and it's time to show ID. Here's what I want my brothers to understand. This test would have eventually come, with or without #ForeverDuncan.

Every relationship has a test point when cards are placed on the table, and you really get to see if this person is for you or not. Some people ignore the test, and some people ignore the results of the test. Fellas, it is key that you pay attention to the test and the results of the test. See the test is normally in an area that you have difficulty with and the results reveal how much you've improved or how much you need to improve in that area. The test may seem like it's revealing issues in the relationship, but it's really revealing issues within yourself. It's important that you are completely honest with yourself with both the test and the results. I've come to learn that if you're not honest with yourself, then most likely, you aren't honest with others. If you struggle with being patient with yourself, then you probably have the same issues with others. The same goes for anything else that you may require or desire in a spouse. You must make sure that you are what you are requesting.

This advice is not only for significant others in romantic relationships either. It also applies to friendships. You won't find many long-lasting friendships amongst people who aren't equally yoked. I'm not talking about social status. I'm talking mentally and spiritually yoked.. You are a reflection of the company that you keep. As you grasp this concept, you will begin to inspect all relationships for growth elements. You will no longer want to be around someone who isn't on the same wavelength as you, not because you think you are better than them, but because you think you're better than who you were before. Stay committed to that. Stay committed to the growth of you. The Law of Attraction states that you are what you attract. So if you're constantly working on you, then what do you think will come along in the form of a mate? If you practice this same self-reflection as a couple, then you are on your way to "happily ever after."

The relationship that men have with our significant others are the true example of who and what we are...
- VIC

This relationship is crucial, because it exposes the depths of your soul. Think about it for those who are married. Can anybody make you as angry as your significant other? Can anybody make you as happy as your significant other? For me, there is no one. My wife exists on both of those spectrums, because she loves all of me, and I love all of her. And to truly love somebody, you have to love every ounce of their good and bad.

When they are being annoying, you have to love them. When they woke up on the wrong side of the bed, you have to love them. When they are dealing with death in the family, you have to love them. When they are stressed out at work, you have to love them. Many of us, just deal with surface love. How is this person making me feel at this very moment in time? If we only deal with surface love it can confuse and isolate us. Instead, we should love our spouses like we love ourselves, fully.

Nobody knows your mistakes and your imperfections like you. Think about the love you have for yourself? With all the mistakes you have made in the past, you are still here, still trying to work and improve your situation,

43

and maybe still trying to forgive yourself for certain things that you may have done. But you are still here. You try to treat yourself right, build yourself up, and surround yourself with people who want the best for you. Even though you have done some things in the past that may not have been too productive. **The way we treat ourselves should be the same way we treat our significant others.**

We have to ensure that our spouses are treated with the same level of concern and decency when they make mistakes… when they are going off for no reason at all. How we act in our greatest moments of frustration will dictate how others view us. No one brings out more emotions in you than your significant other, because you give them every one of your emotions.

One day I asked my 8-year-old son, "Do you think I treat your mother right?" He responded, "Yeah, you guys don't fight, and you don't scream at her." Initially, I felt real good about myself. I felt like I was providing a positive example to my son on how to treat a woman, but then I thought a little more deeply. Am I really showing him? I have been married for 11 years. To say we have never screamed at each other or had a heated verbal disagreement would be so far from the truth. So what my son saw was half the story.

He never saw the late night conversations, the tears shed when being committed to growth, the apologies, the self-reflection, the dedication, the money management, the sacrificing, the setbacks, the support through family members dying, the grind to continue to push through. After that conversation with my son, my wife and I had a discussion to decide what to expose him to. We agreed that we needed to begin exposing him to "decent disagreements." We want him to know that **being committed to someone is not all good but it is all worth it.** We want him to know that when you are trying to build a family you are going to have some bumps, but you must be sure that you continue to work on yourself first and you will be an amazing reflection for your wife.

I always dreamed of raising a boy...
- Black

I had this idea that he would be a split image of me physically and mentally. I had this idea that he would love almost everything that I love and would want me to teach him all that I know. As you already know, you may have a dream, but God has a purpose for you that trumps your dream. So instead of having a son who is a splitting image of me, God gave me a son that is completely himself with little interest in the things that I love. God doubled up on me and gave me a nephew who is also unapologetically himself, with just a minor interest in the things that I love. Fatherhood is easily the toughest job that I've ever taken on. It would be much easier if I birthed a child who shared my same interests, desires and goals. I wouldn't have to learn a thing in order to help him grow. But of course that's never the case.

My son and nephew constantly challenge my knowledge in areas I've never ventured. I've grown to love this about them. See I grew up knowing that I was different than most of my peers. I had different cares and concerns. I moved differently, I thought differently. I accepted this about myself, because I was loved differently. My mother never pushed anything on me. She would give me advice, but would always encourage me to make my own decisions. She wouldn't try to sway me one way or the other. What she would do was sit me down and make me evaluate the situation for myself. She required me to make decisions based on my train of thought. Once I made said decision, she would support it to the fullest. If I succeeded, she would celebrate with me and tell me what she thought I did right and what she thought I did wrong. If I failed, she would lift me up, dust me off, and make sure that I learned whatever lesson I needed to learn through the failed attempt. This was so crucial for my growth. At an early age, I was granted the gift of failure. Yup, I said the gift of failure. I learned that there was no way that I would succeed in every attempt. But I should learn a lesson from every attempt.

This lesson would help me tweak some things for my next attempt. My mother knew that learning how to fail good was a big key to growth so she allowed it to happen. Of course she could've led me away from danger, but how would that have helped me in the long run? Most people try their best to shield their children from any and all danger. I think that is reckless parenting, and those people are creating a false sense of success in their children by doing this. These parents create a learning deficit for important life lessons. I'm not saying that parents should not intervene when a child is making a decision that is detrimental to his/her future and or health. However, parents should practice a level of discernment that protects the child, but helps him/her grow as an individual.

Is there a greater frustration than helping an 8-year-old with homework?

- VIC

Is there any sadness greater than watching your child fail at something that they really want? Is there any pain greater than watching your child in physical or emotional suffering? I don't care if you are a 6'6, 250-pound super diesel dude or not. Those examples will break you down. Straight rip you to shreds! **Fatherhood is tough, but it's so necessary to deal with all of those emotions.** Far too often, men are taught that they have to tough and rough their way through every situation, without taking some time to pay attention to their personal feelings. Yes fellas, I said "feelings." Yes brother, you do have them. No matter how much we try to repress them, they are there and contrary to popular belief, it is just fine to move through these feelings, but it is not always the best practice to act on them. Feelings are great, but take some time. Let those emotions move through you before making decisions with your children.

My son and I were in the barbershop recently. He had just finished getting his haircut and I was in the chair. While he was in the chair, I took some time to proofread his book report. While I was reading it, I noticed myself becoming instantly frustrated, because I saw that he wasn't working to his full potential. By the time he was finished in the chair, I was more settled, because I was able to call my wife and vent. As I was getting in the chair, I gave him the instructions I thought he needed to correct all the mistakes that I spotted. I sent him to a corner in the barbershop to finish his assignments. Three minutes later, he came back to me like he was finished. While he was walking up, I immediately became frustrated, because I knew he didn't spend the time he needed to make sure the report was accurate. All the frustration from earlier came rushing back, coupled with some added threats if the assignment was not to my liking. By the time we left the barbershop, the report was not close to being complete, but when we got into the car to leave, I gathered my feelings, organized my thoughts, and I stopped making the report about me and transitioned the outcome to be about him. I said, "Is this your best work? Have you truly taken the time necessary for this to be work that you would be proud to put your name on? Have you put the same amount of energy into this report as you do in other areas of your life? I would like for you to take some time to put all of your energy into this assignment and then let's celebrate the outcome together. I will help you make some enhancements when you finish giving your all." By the time we arrived at our next desti-nation, the report was complete and he felt success.

That was an example of one success. I have not han-dled every situation with that level of care and concern, but that is a good example to explain how we should handle our moments of frustrations. I could have decided to act out my frustration and anger. I could have screamed, placed blame and even struck him. But instead, this time I chose to breathe, reflect and guide my son. This approach yielded more positive results while also giving my son character tools he could use as he matriculates into manhood. Far too often, we do what's easy in fatherhood. We often mask every feeling except anger and then quickly act on this emotion. The ways in which we consistently treat and teach our children will define who they become. We can be stern, but we should also show love. What we say in love does matter, but what we do in love is what matters the most. So just like we forgive ourselves when we make mistakes, we must do the same for the children we love. We must love them as we love ourselves.

When your child asks, "Daddy, you want to race down the street? I think I can beat you." Say nothing at all except, "On your mark, get set, go!" and smoke them! And when you beat them, let them know, "You are racing your father. You are currently inferior to me physically. Keep working and I am sure you will beat me one day." I have never let my son beat me in anything in an effort to make him feel good. That creates a false sense of pride. If children want to win at life, they have to learn to work for it. They will take losses. They will feel bad, but it's important that they can identify the feeling and be aware of how to work through it. Loving our children does not mean that we have to save our children from pain, losses or heartache. Our jobs as fathers, is to help guide them through the tough parts of their lives. As a result, they will be able to effectively manage the highs and lows that come with living a full life.

1. You can't truly love your community if you don't make an effort to understand our collective situation and history as Black men.
2. Manhood = Service.

CHAPTER V.

COMMUNITY

←—————————————————————————→

I've always lived in impoverished neighborhoods.
- Black

You know the type of neighborhoods where there are a whole bunch of 'youngins' outside at all times of the night—smoking and drinking and laughing at each other? Some were selling drugs and some were out there just because "the strip" was the place to be. I was one of the folks that were just out there because it was the place to be. See I was an athlete and an artist. Because of my abilities, the D-boys wouldn't let me get in on the drug game. They thought I had a future, so they kept me away from their business.

However, we still shared each other's company on a regular basis. I remember countless adults walking pass us and not saying one word. No "Hello." No "What's up?" No "What y'all doing out here?" No nothing. They would just walk pass like they were too good to speak... like they were better than the youth that took over their own parking lots. Mind you, this group of youth was filled with people from different walks of life. But yet they lumped us all together and labeled all of us "problem children." There would be some adults that spoke every single time. They were well respected in the neighborhood. We would make sure nobody sat on their car. If it was a woman, we would make sure somebody carried her grocery bags to the door when she got home from the store. We respected them so much that we would never curse or litter in front of them.

This respect came from just regular ole greetings. These greetings would eventually open up conversations and conversations would lead to understanding and respect. Once you have understanding and respect, you now have the ability to change a person's life. You now have trust and another whole world opens up. You now have the person's attention, whether that person is a child or an elderly adult. If this person is a child, you now have an open doorway to begin pouring into his/her life and molding them to take a positive path in life. It is our duty as men to pour into our community with love and to serve our youth with compassion and commitment.

One day, my son and I were waiting to get our haircuts, when the entire barber shop erupted in a passionate discussion about who is the best football team and who would win that week's game...
- VIC

Everyone was so passionate and loud that my 8-year-old son tried to join the conversation. Before he parted his lips, I gestured to him that we can allow them to engage in the conversation without us because it had no grounding. I wasn't bothered that a bunch black men were relaxing in the shop enjoying sports. But I was bothered that just a few days prior, a few innocent Black men were murdered by police officers. I was bothered that sports like football and basketball are one of few topics that breed passion. In my mind, I was trying to figure out why these brothers weren't as passionate about and intensely debating what steps were needed to end police violence against people of color. **I wanted to figure out why all these grown men were not trying to enlighten the young men in the barbershop on how to defend their humanity in the streets.**

One great thing about the advent of social media is that it allows for people to share their opinions with the world, but it also allows people who are ill-informed the same access. I think it would be an amazing idea for men to challenge each other intellectually rather than just in sports conversation. I want us to begin to understand why we think and act the way we do. If we truly love our communities we will make an effort to start learning substantive information to ensure that we are working and sharing something of value with our young people.

Community service is much more than sharing a laugh over an argument in a barbershop. Providing a service means that you have something that can help another person. For men to truly serve their communities we must first have something to give. That starts with knowing more than what is put in front of you online or on television. We have to learn *and unlearn* important information so that we can help to guide a new generation of powerful, enlightened and compassionate warriors.

PART 2.
LEADERSHIP

CHAPTER VI.

DAILY DECISIONS
DEFINE LEADERSHIP

The toughest decision is always the best...
-VIC

I am currently in my sixth year as a vice principal at a middle school in Maryland. One day when I was on hallway duty, one of my male students walked past me with his pants below his waist. As he was walking, I stopped him, gave him a five and asked him, "Do you think I'm a man?" He quickly responded, "Yeah." I followed with, "Do you ever see me with my pants sagging like that?" He immediately went to pull his pants up, but I stopped him and said, "You don't have to pull your pants up for me." I continued, "You seemed pretty quick to pull them up. Why do you sag them anyway?" He said, "I don't have a belt." "You want one of mine?" I asked. As he walked away he responded, "Nah, I only wear designer belts." The following day I saw him walking down the hallway. He stopped me, pointed to his waist and said, "Brother Victorious, I have a belt today." I smiled with pride as he walked past, but then he turned and whispered, "It's Gucci though." This is a fine example of what leadership looks like. **We must all live by example, not by just our words.** It is ultra important for us not to lead by shaming others, but rather, we must lead by inspiring others. Our lives must be attractive and inviting to those closest to us.

I know you've heard the term, "The magic happens outside of your comfort zone..."

- Black

If you have not heard that term, then you're welcome. It's true though. Comfort is the enemy of growth. When you get comfortable, you tend to stop learning. Most of the time we are comfortable when our lives are based on habit. Habit doesn't take any thought. It's just an action that's embedded in your head and is performed unconsciously most of the time. Comfort is the enemy of success. Comfort will make you suppress the fact that you want more out of your life. Comfort will keep you in a relationship that's going nowhere. In my city, we use the term, "Jump out there." When used correctly, it means that someone did something bold that requires some kind of reaction. Example: "I wasn't even talking to slim. I was talking to my girl. Instead of minding his business, he decided to JUMP OUT THERE and open his mouth so I had to bust his ass." So many people are scared to jump out there, because they don't want to get their ass busted. I feel you though. No one wants to get their ass busted. But truth be told, we all will get our ass busted multiple times in our lives. Manhood is knowing the potential consequences but jumping out there anyway.

There are no shortcuts to manhood.
- Black

I am the type of driver that will try my best to find the quickest route to any location. I will even challenge the accuracy of the GPS, even though it has carefully calculated my travel down to an exact time of arrival. So what, I don't believe it. I think I can get there faster. I always lose this battle. Like most men, I am wired to go and go fast. Unlike the GPS, we didn't take into consideration the traffic, the traffic lights, the accident at the midpoint or the speed limit of the streets. I don't even have access to all the information that my GPS has, and yet I still think I know a shorter route. Some of us approach manhood with the same impatient attitude. We want what we want, when we want it, and most of the time, the "when" is now. Manhood is a process like everything else that takes effort. A lot of us just stumble upon manhood.

Some of us don't have a GPS in the form of a father or a male role model who have traveled this road once before. We were just pointed in the direction of manhood and were told to go find it. It's like we were thrown in the game with no experience and or reference point on how to win the game. The thing is, if you stay committed to the game then you will learn along the way. You will have many loses, however you will gain a plethora of knowledge. I can't tell you how long you may lose along the way, but you will win mini battles occasionally. Hopefully your victory with these mini battles will encourage you to keep going. This is what you were built for. You will learn how to take losses and keep it moving. It is your responsibility to learn from these loses and help the next generation move faster to manhood then you did. Trust the process, and note that you are going through what you are going through to help someone else through their process. If you take short cuts, then inevitably you are cutting someone short of their journey to manhood.

MAN UP-LIFTING

One of my best friends once told me that being a man simply means that you are able to eat a "shit sandwich" and not complain about it.

- VIC

Oftentimes, others won't have extreme concern about how you feel. Being a man means that you are able to lead anyway. As a leader, there is no one to complain to and you won't always be understood by the people who you are serving, but that does not mean that you should stop leading. Our daily decisions are the true determinant of our leadership. Our consistency is what builds our authenticity. As a leader, you will not be perfect. And when you make big mistakes you will pay for them, but there are no shortcuts to manhood. **You have to endure the struggles that come along with life in order to fully serve as an inspiration to others.** It is not just our successes that inspire others to lead, but it is sometimes the long road of healing. We must possess the ability to be vulnerable in our toughest moments. Understand that manhood is a journey that all of us will spend a lifetime trying to reach, because there are no shortcuts. Everyday brings more growth.

Remember, it's almost never about you. Doing for others is doing for yourself (I am we).

Popular men in media are promoting a lie that it's possible to be "self made..."

- VIC

I get instantly bothered whenever I hear someone utter those words. **How is it humanly possible to be a "self-made" man?** Everything that we are is a collection of the communities that raised us, the good and the bad. Along the way, there were people who provided us with good and bad advice that we had to consider. If it weren't for others sharing their lives and experiences with us, none of us would be who and what we are. And because there were plenty who helped create us, we must ensure that we do the same for others as they progress into manhood. To celebrate a life of being "self-made" automatically promotes a narcissistic self absorbed life. Instead, men should have their minds focused on how they can help others. Who truly cares about your professional, academic or financial pursuits if they have not helped or benefited people other than you? We can easily begin to buy into this false narrative that manhood is defined by how much money you have or how much status you have acquired. We should focus on being community made, not self-made.

The pursuit of recognition is mental slavery...
- Black

Trying to be recognized takes away the freedom of you just being you. When you try to appease others by your actions then you are no longer being real with yourself. You are no longer being the true you. The true you is who you are destined to be. The great you is who you should strive to be. No one should seek recognition for the pursuit of being the best person he should be. The reward is always the results. The results are not just a reward for you but a reward for everyone that comes in contact with you. Truth be told, your greatest you is not about you at all. God allowed you to grow into this person because he wants you to touch the world. It was never about you to begin with. It was about you being a testimony to others so that they can seek the best them.

Within these last three years I have changed immensely. My spirit has changed. My outlook on life has changed. My view of manhood has changed. I felt the change happening, but I was the person changing, so I never really gave much thought to it. I really started paying attention to the change when I recognized that others started changing around me, because of my change. Some of my friends and co-workers would try to be the best them in front of me. I never asked for this, and at times, I would feel uncomfortable because I thought they were putting me on some kind of pedestal and I didn't want that responsibility. I would often say, "I am just like you slim. I have some of the same demons you have. You don't have to change in front of me." Not knowing that they weren't changing because of me, but they were changing because of the change they saw in me. I didn't have anything to do with it. It wasn't about me at all. It was about what was done to me that inspired them to want the same. Manhood is never about you. It is always about what and who you inspire. Your legacy won't be based on what you have accumulated, but more so, about what you have given away.

Being a man is difficult. Stop complaining…
- Black

Prior to #ForeverDuncan, I was a case manager for a company that assisted welfare recipients in getting employment and/or education to acquire employment. I was super excited to be working with folks that I thought got the short end of the stick in this thing we call life. I quickly learned that it would be more headaches than triumphant moments in the career field that I chose. It was very difficult to get some of my clients to participate in the program. Frustration quickly formed, because my performance was based on the amount of people I could get to participate in the program. Because of my personality, I had a lot of success in convincing my clients to participate. I was so successful that management thought that it would be a good idea to give me a batch of clients who were considered to be non-compliant and uninterested, with hopes that I could work my magic and bring them in.

At first they created a new flow chart that would give me extra support to achieve the task they expected me to do. Then all of a sudden, they decided not to change the process and left me with a caseload filled with people that other case managers didn't want. I was pissed to say the least. For about two weeks, I came in the office with an attitude. I didn't enjoy my fellow co-workers. I didn't enjoy my work space and most of all, I didn't enjoy my work. Relationships with my clients took a turn for the worst. I started resenting them for making me work harder than anyone in the building, in my opinion. I dreaded waking up and going to the office. I'm not normally a negative type of guy so others noticed my attitude and would often point it out to me. After a while, the situation at work started to effect my household. I would bring my frustrations home. My wife (then girlfriend) would be irritated because I wasn't the pleasant guy that she fell in love with. Eventually I realized that my complaining wasn't helping my job and it was damaging my relationships with those around me. I then began to think of a solution to my problem. I created an outreach system that focused on constant communication and accountability between my clients and I.

I created tools to assist me with the day-to-day execution of my plan to solve this problem. I was excited again. It showed in my work. It showed in my spirit. It showed in my health and it showed in my relationships. Things started to flourish because I was focused on solving problems and not on complaining about problems. They eventually promoted me to outreach manager and assigned two employees to assist with my efforts. I went from an angry case manager to an essential part of bettering a business. Wow. I learned a lot about manhood during this process. In my opinion, manhood is about solving problems. If your focus is on solving a problem, then you rarely have time to complain. You were designed to be an asset and not a burden when it comes to problem solving. Men are driven by figuring out stuff. Most of the time, we don't even accept help because there is so much joy in figuring things out by ourselves. Tap into that. If there is a need and you fill the void, you will feel so accomplished even if you aren't acknowledged for it. Manhood is difficult, however, you have all the tools to acquire it. There will be plenty of tough days in which you fail at your goal, but there is no time for complaining. So Man-Up and do the work. Don't focus on the fruit of your labor, because the labor is the fruit when it comes to manhood.

I remember a few years back, I was going through an extremely rough patch in my marriage...
- VIC

I felt like my wife was treating me unfairly, and I was constantly complaining about the wrongs that I felt she was doing. The complaints only led to me being further frustrated. This caused me to ignore how my own actions could be contributing to my own frustrations. My complaints were the fuel for my frustration, rather than an expression. My complaints actually supported and grew my issues. During those times, I learned a lot about how the words I speak can contribute to my own unhappiness and how it can stunt my growth.

If you are one of those manly man dudes, this is really going to sound soft to you. Instead of complaining, men, we need to do a better job at expressing our feelings. Identifying how situations make us feel is the key, not how we talk about other people's actions. When I started to recognize and speak to my feelings, I was able to change my verbal responses and my misguided actions. Connecting with our feelings instead of complaining will guide us into growing into powerful men.

CHAPTER VII.

MAN OF THE HOUSE

Who really makes the final decision?
- VIC

Men are always faking like we are in charge! You ain't in charge homie, especially if you married. Men always holding onto this idea that they are the commander-in-chief because it makes them feel good. And a good wife knows that even though they are secretly making the decisions, it is important to let a man think that he is.

The most sexist belief on earth is to think that our marriages can only be productive if we, men, are in charge. This idea stems from our own insecurities related to manhood. The age old belief is that domination is power and submission is weakness. This is absolutely false. Domination and submission should be equally exchanged in a mutual relationship. There will be times in which the man in a relationship should take the lead, and there should be times when the woman takes the lead. This idea that men are the only people who should rule in a relationship is false, and it only leads to unnecessary power struggles that can ultimately cause tension in marriage.

You should make final decisions together, and there should be an equal exchange of power based on the situation and circumstance. And when in doubt, always, let her make the final decision. Your life will be better for it.

I often submit to my wife publicly.

-Black

Most of the time it's in a playful type of way, but underneath it all she really runs shit. I ain't gonna fake with you and act all macho about it. My wife's happiness is key in my household. If you don't believe me, you can ask my son. I could have a terrible day and come home with an attitude and the only person who will cater to me is my wife. My son wouldn't be tripping and my stepdaughter would trip a little bit, but she will get over it very quickly. But if my wife comes in the house with a bad attitude then it will affect the entire mood of the household. Because of this alone, she really runs shit. I may be the man of the house, but it is my duty as the man of the house to make sure the house is in a good space and most of the time, that means making sure my wife is in a good space. You know the saying, "Happy wife, happy life."

Now don't get it twisted. My wife can't just come in with an attitude about something stupid and expect me to jump through hoops to make her feel better. Nah, that's not gonna work. I have to hold her accountable to creating positive vibes in our home. If she is being ridiculous then as "man of the house" I am responsible for showing her the mirror and encouraging her to get herself together. As I stated in previous chapters, manhood isn't really about you.

It's more so about how you solve problems and ensure that everything works in accordance with the bigger goal. In my household, I try to help make decisions that would alleviate any future problems because that means less work for me in the future. You sir, are the clean-up man of the house. There lies the difference.

Sacrifice
1. Men forgo their wants to ensure their family's needs are in tact.

All I ever want to do is go on vacation…
- VIC

I would be satisfied if I could travel to another state or country at least once a month. Not only do I want this, I actually make plans in my mind about how I can do this often. I'm a live-for-the-moment kind of guy. If I work hard, I think I should be able to treat myself. And traveling is my escape from the daily hustle and bustle, the bills and responsibilities, the sacrifice and dedication. The only problem is that traveling is expensive and if I traveled the way I wanted to, I would be neglecting the needs of my family.

I've learned that for me it is best practice to identify my needs, but then to quickly understand that they don't matter. The only needs that matter are my family's. If I move from that space, then it is a pretty good chance that my needs will begin to matter to everyone else. In my few years of manhood, I noticed that when I am selfless, my needs are satisfied.

My gratification as a man is related directly to the spiritual, physical, and financial security of my family. Which means, I must be present as much as possible. The great majority of my income should benefit my family, not just myself, and I have to be very much a part of the spiritual guidance of my family.

I've learned that my family's security should always be my primary need, my personal fulfillment

should always be secondary. Though this can sometimes be a tough thing to do considering I am a human being, this approach has been the most effective for me. This is not to say that we should forgo satisfying ourselves. However, we should put family first.

When it comes to fashion, I'm super fly in my head...
- Black

For real I am. I really think that I have fashion sense, and I could possibly be the best dressed person in the world if I had the money to purchase clothes. You are probably laughing, but I am for real. Okay, let me humble myself. Maybe not the world, but at least a small portion of the world. Like about three to four zip codes. Nobody would be able to out dress me in the 83201. You don't have to look that up, that's the zip code for Bannock County, Idaho. Lol. The way my life is set up, I don't have the money to purchase the fly things that I see. I'm not talking about expensive clothes either. I don't need labels to look good. My budget is very attracted to Ross, Marshalls and T.J. Maxx— especially the ones in the Caucasian neighborhoods. They always have a better selection, because no one is really shopping there and if they are, they aren't necessarily looking for the clothes that I like.

You are probably thinking, 'Damn, you don't have the money to ball out at T.J. Maxx? Well I do have the money to pop tags at T.J. Maxx, however I have more important things to do with my money. Those things include making sure that my family's needs are taken care of. But don't get it twisted. I still stay fly out here in these streets, but not before I make sure that my family stays fly in our home.

CHAPTER VIII.

COMMUNITY

←——————————————————————————→

Contribution is key.
1. If there is a need, fill it.
2. Being "community-oriented" means more than just posting a Facebook Status (it's more than Social Status).

Whether we like it or not we are all role models…
- VIC

It's so easy to cop out of our roles and scream, "I ain't no role model!" When people say this, what they really mean is, "I don't want to be responsible for anything." Our responsibilities extend beyond taking care of just our immediate families. Though I believe that our homes should be our primary responsibility, I do not believe that it stops there. Our communities and communities around the world are in desperate need of help from solid men. Considering everything happening with our youth during these times, if you are not an active participant in the creation of positive change, then you are an active part of the problem.

Young people in our communities are looking for guidance and if you are an able-minded man who does not sacrifice your time to ensure that young people have a solid foundation, then you are a part of the problem.

As it is widely understood, the family structure in some of our communities are not fully intact, partly because unfortunately many men have confused abandonment with independence, and have dipped out on their responsibilities. It feels like the moment things get rough for us and cease to be just entertainment, many men choose to leave... as if, manhood should just be fun.

Manhood is tough and we are dealing with harsh realities in our communities. If we do not step up to the plate real soon, things will quickly move from bad to worse. Though educating the world through a Facebook status, Instagram meme or Tweet can be helpful, it is not enough to create substantial change. If we are to change our communities, we have to begin to put feet to pavement and arms of love around individuals who are hurting. We MEN are a collection of those who raised us, and we have a responsibility to be that same community for the young people who are currently growing up.

I have a buddy who decided to start coaching youth football a couple of years ago...
- Black

Coincidentally, he was coaching my son's age group. Of course my friend asked me if my son wanted to play on his team. My son didn't really want to play football, but I thought he needed the camaraderie and skills that team sports teach, so I 'kinda' forced him to play. He gave me a hard time on our way to his first practice so I made a deal with him. "If you don't have fun during this first practice, then you don't have to play. But you can't go in here with an attitude. You have to give it your all." He agreed. We pulled up to practice, and he joined the team on the field. I stayed in my car and watched from a distance, because I did not want to distract him. As I was watching the team, certain things were irking the hell out of me. See, I played Little League sports from the age of 6 all the way up to 13. I learned a lot about manhood while playing on these teams. I learned a lot about dedication and commitment. I learned a lot about work ethic and sacrifice. Little League had a big impact on my adulthood, so of course I got irritated when I noticed the kids goofing off when the coach's head was turned the other way. I got out of my car and walked over to the field just to show the 'youngins' that they had another set of eyes on them. Some of them straightened up, but some of them did not care. I stared down the ones that didn't care and they eventually got the message, but as soon as I turned away from them, they would go back to goofing off. "Are these little punks challenging me?" I thought in my head. At that I moment, I started my Little League coaching career. Man I gave them an earful, and I'm sure they were thinking, "Who the hell is this guy? "Who me, I'm Coach Black." See manhood would not allow me to stand idle while kids were goofing off and wasting time with an opportunity that I knew could impact their growth in a positive way. At first, I did not want to volunteer to take on this coaching job, because I knew it would be a serious time commitment that I didn't feel I could spare, but when I saw the situation with my own eyes, how could I not help? I had the knowledge, ability and passion to influence the kids . How could I not fill that void? Sure, I didn't have a lot of time to offer them, but I had enough time to make an impact.

Never forget, you must "love" your child and all children you can influence.
1.   Speak life into all youth.
2.   Don't be afraid to lead. (Your words won't matter if you don't follow up with actions.)
3.   Your presence makes a bigger impact than you think.

Have you ever received a soft handshake from a person who could not look you in the eyes?
- VIC

When a group of powerful, educated and astute Black men enter a room, there is no denying our presence. It speaks volumes before we say one word. That same presence speaks volumes when we come home and greet our children or when we are interacting with our communities. However, I have met plenty brothers who are super massive in stature, but have absolutely no presence.

Recently, I was walking with my son through the toy aisle at Target. He wanted to spend $26 of the birthday money he had just received before it burned a hole in his pocket. As I was following my 8-year-old through the same toy aisle over and over again, I saw this other young brother about the same age as my son playing one of the sample game consoles in the video game section. I only noticed him because he was talking to the game that he was playing. I thought he was having a dope time because he seemed like he was very into it. But then I heard this little brother say, "Fuck this!"

Initially, I thought, *I must be hearing things, I know this young dude didn't say that?* A couple seconds later, he said, "Shit, this game cheating like hell!" So, look, I'm slightly immature. So once I knew he said it, I slightly chuckled under my breath, but then I got it together. I walked over to him, looked him in the eye and said, "Aye, young King, you cursing over here?" By the time I could get my next sentence out, he let go of the controller and took off! Super fast!

He took off, not because he felt threatened or because I used harsh words towards him, I believe he ran away because he realized that he was in the presence of a man. It felt like he was not use to the feeling or the energy of men, but he did respect it.

When I returned to my son, he said, "Dad, did you just say something to that boy about cursing?" I nodded. He continued, "He is going to be mad." I replied, "King, I'm no superman, but it's important to me that we all guide when we can. **If you were in a store cursing I would want someone to discipline you as well.** I am a part of the village." He nodded and said no more, and continued to look for his $26 treasure.

When I reflect on this experience, I see a lot of take-aways. First, I think I showed the young king playing the game a strong reinforcement of male presence and love. It is important for able-minded men to show up for our young people when they are asking for our attention. Just as in the case of this young brother, a child may ask for attention in a variety of ways, but it is up to us to ensure that we are attentive and present. Secondly, I think my son was able to gain an understanding of his role in his community and how he should work to maintain his behavior and integrity while in and out of my presence.

Lastly, it was a lesson for me to remain mature, but to remember to keep pushing forward and have no worries about repercussions. In that moment when I spoke to the young king, I wasn't thinking about how his guardians would respond. I was trying to do what was right. Most times when we focus on doing the right thing, the great majority of the time, the right thing will happen for us.

The Washington Metropolitan Area Transit Authority, or the Metro as we call it here in the DMV, can definitely be a social test of patience for adults...

- Black

This is especially true on certain train and bus routes that travel through "The Hood." The 'youngins' on the train seem to have no respect for adults as a whole. The conversations that they have in the open would make you think there is no one on the Metro except them. What amazes me even more is that no one ever steps up and says anything to them. It's like all the adults are scared to speak up. What the hell changed? When I was young, my friends and I would have never been able to get away with this. Someone, if not everyone, would have stepped up and put us in our places. Not only would they step up to discipline us, they would also step up to encourage us. I don't see much of that anymore.

A lot of us blame the youth for their lack of respect. Most adults think that a great percentage of our young Kings and Queens are a lost cause and there is no way to get through to them, so they don't bother trying to school them. Adults just ignore them and act like they don't care. Well, if we really look in the mirror, the ownest is on us adults. I have a 12-year-old son and a 5-year-old stepdaughter. My step daughter is quite mature for her age, but often she reminds me that she is just five. My son is 12, and although he may act immature from time-to-time, he is 12 and I have to hold him to that level of maturity. So if my son and my step-daughter get in an argument, my son must always maintain his level of maturity. It may not always feel fair to him, but his age gives him a bigger responsibility. He can take more than she can and I expect him to. He can also be an example for her which can potentially help her to mature faster. The same can be said for all these adults walking around here turning their noses up at our misguided youth. You are grown. These kids grow up under your tutelage.

If they are a mess, it's because they came from a mess. That *mess* would be "us" as a whole. You know why they don't care? Because we collectively don't show them that we care. You would be surprised how receptive a young person would be if you pulled him/her aside and spoke life and love into them while correcting them on their current behavior. But nah, we have our own kids to worry about right? Or we are just too exhausted from all of our "adulting" that we don't have time to help a child that isn't ours? Man-Up slim. I remember when the youth were rioting in Baltimore because Freddie Gray was murdered by police. (That wasn't a typo).

Facebook went crazy with youth bashing. I was so upset over what I was reading. I couldn't believe the things that people were saying about a group of children who were clearly frustrated with the treatment that their community was receiving by so-called community servants who are paid to serve and protect. Did we forget that children act out when they feel they are being mistreated? Did we also forget that we are supposed to be their protectors and leaders? SMH. Let me step off of my soap box for a minute. So the next day, Victorious, the co-author of this book, called me up and asked me to go with him to Baltimore to walk the streets with the 300 Men Organization. I said "Hell yeah." So Vic, Truth (Vic's brother and my friend) and I drove to Baltimore to meet up with the men that organized this initiative. I didn't know what to expect. I honestly thought we were going to be marching and protesting in the areas of Baltimore that had the heaviest media presence. Nope.

What we did that day will stay with me for the rest of my life. We walked to every hood in Baltimore that had no media presence. We filled the streets with the presence of MANHOOD. People came out to greet us as if we were super heroes. We were welcomed on every block with claps and cheers. What touched me the most was the excitement on kids' faces. They had never seen anything like that before. We took the time to talk to as many kids as possible. We let them know that we were doing this for them. They were ecstatic to know that they meant that much to us. We probably walked a half marathon that day and although my feet were aching when we got back to the car, that march was probably some of the best steps I've ever taken. Man Up = Step Up.

PART 3.
LOYALTY

CHAPTER IX.

INTEGRITY

←――――――――――――――――――――――――――→

Who are you when nobody is watching?
- VIC

Now being loyal to yourself is probably one of the most difficult aspects of manhood. I mean, it's sometimes super hard. Loyalty is synonymous with consistency and consistency is the most difficult thing to maintain. Consistency means something happens every day. You demonstrate consistent integrity through every decision that you make, which is a challenge to even think about. **I truly believe that how you manage your integrity is what makes you into the man that you are and will become**. As a growing man, though it's tough for me to admit, this is an area that I have struggled with the most. I have struggled because I have been selfish. There were times throughout my journey as a man when the only person I truly thought about was myself... so much so, that I ultimately began to display narcissistic tendencies. This realization led me into a very deep sadness and ultimately into a depressive state. In order to overcome, I had to seek help from a therapist. Yep, a certified, bonafide, therapist! And nope, I ain't crazy.

Well, maybe a little bit, but I am only discussing this because I want to bring some normality to speaking with a therapist. Let's face it, manhood is difficult, and if you are a man of color, it ups the ante even more. Without the proper support and guidance, we will act out and begin to destroy everything that we worked so hard to build. We need to do a better job at thinking about why we believe what we believe. We have to dismantle the stigma that there is shame in speaking with someone honestly and fully about what happens to us mentally, emotionally and spiritually.

I truly believe that seeking help from a therapist saved my life. It helped me to see that many of my shortcomings were self-inflicted. I learned that in order to grow and develop, there were things that I had to let go of, including friends that I had to sideline and experiences that I had to pause. Without a careful examination of my life, I wouldn't be on a path of awareness. I specifically say "path" because manhood is a constant journey. We make decisions daily. In order to continue to make the decisions that make me most successful, I have to continue to surround myself with people, places and things that will aide in my integrity to evolve.

If you are ever embarrassed because your behavior or thoughts were revealed to the world without your approval, then you should recognize that you have some changing to do.

- Black

If your actions make you self-conscious and uncomfortable, those feelings are an indication that you have an opportunity to better yourself. Self-reflection is key to this type of growth. The emphasis here is on the word "self." It is very important that you are true to who you are regardless of who is watching. It makes for a more peaceful life. People are going to judge you regardless, but if you are truly happy with your decisions, then the judgement doesn't bother you much, sometimes not at all. We constantly throw the phrase around "Keep it 'ahunit.'" (That means *100* for those outside of the hood.) We also say, "Keep it real." These phrases are used in my community to state that what one is saying is truthful as possible with whomever the audience is at that time. Let's keep it *'100.'* No one keeps it *'100'* with anybody besides God. And truth be told, the only reason we keep it *'100'* with God is because He knows everything about us, not because we voluntarily give Him information on our thoughts and actions. This really hit home for me in my senior year of college. It was finals week, and I was swamped with studying, only because I am a super procrastinator. I was struggling in my criminal justice class and I had to get a B grade or higher in order to graduate. I stayed up all night trying to memorize what I thought I needed to know in order to ace the test. Around 4 o'clock in the morning, I realized that there was no way I was going to pull this off. I was so scared that I would fail and that this class would keep me from graduating. Need I mention that I already sent out graduation invitations to my family and they were super excited because I would be the first male to graduate college on both sides of my family.

Fear led me to doing something that I was uncomfortable with, but I thought that it was my last and only resort. We were allowed to have drinks in my class, so I created a cheat sheet and taped it on the back side of the soda label. "Genius," I thought. I was so excited that I showed my basketball teammates. They laughed me out, but gave me props because it was creative. I did mention this was a criminal justice class right? Oh, but I didn't mention that the professor was a retired police officer/private investigator.

So I'm sure you know how this ended. I got caught. I was so embarrassed. I remember having a meeting with the professor and the dean, and I went into straight punk mode. I was crying like I was about to die. I was begging and pleading for them to allow me to make up the test. I was trying my best to gain sympathy from them. They were so disappointed, because they thought that they had a good outlook on my character. I was an intricate member of the basketball team. I was an unspoken leader on campus. I was friends with everybody, so why would they think otherwise. I was so embarrassed by my actions, and no matter how much I pleaded, they wouldn't budge. They said I had to take the course again in order to graduate, which meant that I had to come back an extra semester just for this one course. However, because they held me in high regard, they chose to keep this just between the people in that room. This is the first time that I have ever publicly spoke about this situation. I made up this big lie to my family stating that it was a mix up with my credits, and I had one more class to take, so I wouldn't graduate until the spring semester. I let so many people down that day, but ultimately I let myself down the most. I questioned who I was. Was I just acting "Saint-Like" just to get kudos from folks? Who was I really? Was I the person my professor respected prior to my cheating or was I the person who got caught?

Truth be told, I was both people, however the latter didn't affect me, until I got caught. From that point on, I tried my best to make private decisions that I would be comfortable with publicly. Every decision won't be seen by the public in a good light, but if I'm cool with it, then they don't matter. For instance, I've had my fair share of free cable, and although that may have been seen as stealing, I'm cool with admitting to you that I've had free cable. Man, the cable company has been getting over on us for years. My integrity with myself is intact. We should be questioning their integrity, in my opinion.

How do you treat people who can't do anything for you?

- VIC

    I am originally from Bronx, New York. My mom, followed by my dad, jetted to the DMV when I was about 2-years-old with my two brothers and I. I spent the rest of my years being raised in Prince George's County, MD. Though I lived in Maryland, my family and I would consistently travel to New York to visit my family.

    As a child though, I despised New York City (no offense to the New Yorkers). Everything about it. The smell, the absence of trees, the fast walking, the close spaces, and the lack of backyards. One day I was walking down the street with my amazing aunt Earthly Paradise, and we were approached by a homeless person. The person approached us to ask for something reasonable. Growing up, I thought it was a normal practice to say judgmental things about people who annoyed me. And probably because I was already thrown off by New York culture, I decided to voice my disdain to my aunt, thinking that she would just nod in agreement. Oh was I wrong.

    My aunt began to dismantle my ideas of class and privilege and the shallowness of looking down on people and their experiences. She reminded me to be grateful for what I have, to always remember that things can be swept away from me in an instant. I learned a valuable lesson that day, not just about my treatment of homeless people, but my treatment of people in general.

I learned that I don't know everyone's story, so I have absolutely no right to judge. As I matured, I began to understand that every person deserved the same amount of respect. **No one is more superior than the next, and regardless of title, job or experience, each person deserves to be treated as if God lives inside of them.** As an adult, when a person who may be down on their luck asks me for something, no matter what my response, I take time to look him/her in the eye, slow my pace, and speak in a positive tone. It is my attempt to ensure that I support their humanity. And I am thankful to New York and my amazing aunt for taking the time to teach me such a valuable lesson about manhood.

I have a natural instinct to help people. I get such a thrill out of it...
- Black

There are very few feelings that match the internal satisfaction I receive when I help someone who is in need. In my mind, I am not helping someone in order to receive something in return. But as I re-evaluated this topic, I realized I was wrong. I did want something in return. Not money. Not a thank you. Not recognition. Although those things would be nice, what I wanted was a feeling. A self-gratifying feeling. A feeling of worth. A feeling that I did something good. In my adult life, I know what good looks like, so I don't need anyone to validate it for me. I get a natural high off of this feeling, so I'm always chasing it. The great thing about this is that I can get this feeling from anybody.

You don't have to be in a position to do something for me in order for me to do something for you, because doing something for you already does something for me. It makes me subconsciously pat myself on the back. My son constantly looks for praise from his mother and I. When I tell him "job well done," his face immediately lights up and it confirms in his mind that he is on the right path. I don't believe that feeling ever goes away. The difference between my son and I is that I'm a grown man, and I have a moral compass that holds me accountable for good and bad things I do. So I don't need anyone to tell me, "Job well done." I can tell myself that and when I do, I light up inside, just like my son does.

I have no other friends like Alfred, Mr. #Forever-Duncan...

- VIC

This brother speaks life into me every time we link. He holds me accountable for my decisions and pushes me to the use the gifts that I have been given for good. The brother is all-around dope. **Every man needs a brother in their life who wants the best for you and your family and always tries to steer you in the right direction.**
Alfred has always been that for me. As I grow in my professional experiences, I am learning that being true to what I am built for means that I am ensuring that I am maximizing my gifts. It means that I am not just settling for what is easy, but instead I consider how I can push myself to evolve, to be greater, influence more people, and ultimately serve humanity on a greater scale. If I am going to be true to my purpose and calling, it means that I will be true to the creator. It means that I am always evolving and pushing myself to greater limits.

Everything that I do always involves me creating something...

- Black

I am a creator. I create stuff. That's just what I do. I can't escape it. Even if I am at a 9 to 5 pushing papers, I would probably create a process to make my job easier. That solution would probably come with a spreadsheet and countless other tools. #ForeverDuncan is a prime example of how my mind works. I am not confined to what others think. My mind won't allow me to follow the "rules." There is a quote that I heard during a music theory class in college that I hold on to and revisit often. My professor started off our first class saying, "There are no rules in music, just guidelines." Then she played something that was so unpleasant. She asked everyone if we recognized the sound, and if so, what was it. Everyone instantly yelled out, "Feedback." She asked us for the definition of "feedback," and people began to throw out definitions and all of them correlated. Feedback was believed to be an irritating sound that occurred when something went wrong with the audio equipment. Then she blew my mind. She then played a dope song in which feedback was the catalyst of the song. It was obvious that our definition of "feedback" didn't apply to the song's creator. Feedback was music to him. She then said, "There are no rules to music, just guidelines." Wow. I live by this quote and often refer to it in my daily life, as should you. No one knows you as well as you know yourself. No one can tell you what you were built for. It's up to you to figure it out and pursue it. Be true to it, and don't let anyone steer you away from it. You have been specifically designed to do something amazing. Unfortunately, as hard as it may be for you to see your "amazing," it's even harder for others to see it. Don't let that discourage you. Don't let feedback stop you from making the music.

"Whatever isn't growing is dying." So in essence, life itself is primarily about evolution.

- VIC

I believe that our individual purpose is always the same, but the ways we reach that purpose should be evolving consistently. Our moral foundation is what guides the actions we choose to take daily, but the targets we hope to reach should be interchangeable. **Wandering aimlessly in our careers and personal lives can have an adverse impact on us reaching our goals.** Being strategic and aware of every move we make will ultimately help us to achieve our personal and professional goals.

Remember:
1. Be honest to yourself and others.
2. Don't compromise your loyalty.
3. Trust the process. Joy comes in the morning.

If anyone ever tells you that it's easy to tell the truth, they are probably lying...

- VIC

I guess it's easy to tell the truth when nothing is at stake. I would assume the truth is easier to share when it doesn't evolve around a mistake or shame. **But if we have been through anything or made any mistakes, telling the truth about our shortcomings is probably one of the most difficult things we can do as men.** Honesty requires a hell of a lot of vulnerability and trust. You have to trust that the person you are being honest with will be vulnerable and cautious enough with your feelings not to destroy you. People only lie because they are afraid to face the consequences of the truth. It's difficult to face our demons or the destruction we have caused. But when we decide to, we liberate ourselves and those around us to do the same. We begin to assert our complete selves, flawed and imperfect. When we allow ourselves to trust the process, we begin to understand what love truly is. When we love ourselves, we allow ourselves to go through the pain of growth and development. It allows us to make the crucial decisions regarding our own feelings and emotional development.

In order to live in truth, we have to be examples of how we want to be treated. It is very possible to hold people accountable, while releasing judgement associated with their actions. The truth will begin to flow more loosely when we begin to create judgement free zones for the people we love the most.

The decisions to cut someone off or isolate their presence are still possible without putting labels on the person. Saying, "You are a lying fool, don't ever come around me again!" versus "I am hurt and I am going to create some barriers to remain safe until I am able to regain trust," are received in totally different ways. With a more positive response, the person who lied begins to understand the feelings their actions caused their loved one—they feel convicted not attacked. While at the same time, the person who is hurt presents a possibility and process for trust to be reestablished, versus communicating an empty statement of frustration. If we want people to tell us the truth, we have to foster and exist in an atmosphere of truth.

I had no plans of getting in another relationship with anyone anytime soon.

-Black

When my wife and I started to get to know each other in 2013, I was fresh out of a five year relationship. To be honest, I was really looking forward to the bachelor life. I was about to be a straight smut bucket (promiscuous guy). It was something about my wife that kept me intrigued. I tried my best to keep my distance, but our connection was so strong. I knew I wasn't ready for a relationship though. I knew I was emotionally unavailable, because I was still in love with my ex. Those feelings just don't go away immediately. Although I was still in love with my ex, I wasn't just going to get back with her for the sake of being lonely. And although my wife was a lot of fun and we connected, I wasn't going to run to her just because I was lonely either. I decided to spend some time with myself.

I decided to be loyal to myself. I decided to figure out my needs and make sure I held whoever I dealt with next to those standards. I felt restricted in my past relationship. I felt like I wasn't totally myself, and the person who I was dealing with didn't create a space for me to be all of me. I felt caged in and I wanted to feel free with whomever I decided to settle down with next. I came to the understanding that If I was going to ever get what I wanted in a mate, I would have to be totally honest about my desires and feelings with not only the woman, but also with myself. This isn't a standard practice for manhood according to the unwritten handbook or the examples that I've seen. I've witnessed men lie to women in order to get what they wanted. Most of the time, men lie to get sex. Well, fellas here is a nugget for you. If you are honest with women about your intentions, there is a great chance you will still get what you want. Women respect honesty and honesty is attractive.

Back to my wife and I. Because I'm like that (just playing, but not according to her) my wife fell in love with me within two weeks. I didn't feel the same way about her. I thought she was dope, but I wasn't in love with her. Of course this created awkward situations which required me to be honest even though I knew it would break her heart. One day she told me she loved me. I paused because I was surprised. I gathered myself and looked her straight in her eyes and said, "I would appreciate it if you don't tell me that. It makes me feel uncomfortable." She was pissed. She cussed me out something serious and stormed out of my house. I wasn't 'trippin' because I was honest.

My conscious was clear. I really felt uncomfortable about her telling me that. I felt as if I had to say it back and I wasn't going to say it unless I felt it. So in order to avoid this awkward moment again, I preferred if she didn't say it again. Yeah, I know. Pretty bold. But some things require you to be bold. She was dope, but I was willing to lose her in order to keep my conscious clear. I figured if it was meant to be then it would be. I wasn't 'gonna' trip. I was going to trust the process. This wasn't the first time that she stormed out because of my honesty, and it wouldn't be the last. We would go through this same scenario many times throughout our "getting to know each other" phase, because I stuck to my guns. Every time she left me alone, I felt a sense of pride, because I was just being honest. It was addictive. I was being completely me with no remorse. Every time she left, she came back to me with a different outlook on what she deserved. Once we understood what was happening, we welcomed this process (minus the break-ups) and we've been growing with each other ever since.

CHAPTER X.

MORE THAN JUST A FIST FIGHT

←————————————————————————→

Fights are rare. Guidance is plentiful...
- VIC

One day, I was chilling at home and my best friend called me. When I picked up the phone, his voice sounded frantic as if he was in distress. He said, "What up Vic? Aye my man (who I knew) got into some trouble and I'm about to ride, what up?" If you're from where I'm from, you understand what all this means, but in case you don't understand, let me explain. My best friend had just informed me that one of our mutual friends was in some sort of distress or possible danger and he was about to go help handle the situation (perhaps violently), then he suggested that I go. It wasn't just a suggestion. It also served as a test of my manhood.

One's response in those tense situations are critical. The first thing that came to my mind was that my manhood was being tested. Almost instantly, I started to question everything. Was I being scared or intimidated? If I didn't go, was I not a true friend? But then my rational mind started taking over. I noticed that my best friend called me while I was in the house with my wife and newborn son. I realized that my life was not just about me anymore. I responded, "What's wrong with the brother?" "What type of trouble he in?" "What kind of help does he need?" When I noticed that the answers were abrupt and not detailed enough I swiftly declined. **Putting my life in harm's way for something that I didn't know the details of seemed to be a pretty dumb move.** When I declined, I thought my man would be beefing with me, but he called me the next day and said, "I understand why you said no and there is no respect lost." It was great to know that my best friend respected my decision, but even if he didn't, I was still going to be good either way.

As I have grown and matured, I have begun to understand that friendship is much more than a fist fight. Often times, we base our loyalty on whether or not our man has our back physically, but we forget about all the other ways your homey is supposed to have your back. Is your man having conversations with you about managing your money correctly? Are you encouraging one another as you grow in fatherhood? Are you speaking with one another about being positive spouses? Are you volunteering in your community together? True friendship among men, as adults, almost never involves a fist fight. It does involve our everyday decisions to help grow and develop one another.

In my culture, it's considered unmanly to be a "punk" when it comes to physical altercations...

-Black

Sad enough a part of me believes in this principle as well. So much so that it's a must that my son and nephew know how to defend themselves. I never liked fighting, but of course I had my fair share of fist fights. I won more than I lost, but nonetheless I did take some L's. As I matured, I avoided fights as much as possible. Not because I was scared, although most of the times I was, but because often it was a misunderstanding that could've been settled with a conversation. It's very rare that a confrontation must come to blows, but sometimes it's unavoidable, and I've always been prepared to deal with that. I don't want to deal with it, but there are plenty of things that I don't want to do as a man that I must.

As I grew wiser and developed, I tried to surround myself with like-minded individuals. I tried to surround myself with those who have intelligent conversations that could take days to digest. Those who can change your entire outlook on a particular topic. Those who don't put much value in fighting and would prefer to come home without a scratch or a bruise. It's nothing worst than having a night out with the fellas that gets ruined by a hot head of the group, who always wants to show how tough he is.

Homie we grown, you ain't got nothing to prove. I question that type of friendship, because it presents a danger to my life. I am all the way loyal with my friends, so I need to know that they have my best interests at heart. I am the type of friend who doesn't want to question why I jumped in a fight to defend your honor. Because without question, If I see you are getting pummeled by multiple dudes, I'm jumping in. But if you got me out here looking like a high school kid over something stupid and avoidable, chances are we won't be friends afterwards, and you and I may have our own fight to deal with.

Remember that friends support growth and self-development of their friends.

I didn't have a true de-briefing conversation with my best friend...

- VIC

Luckily he was not in any harm's way, but he should have been considering his wife and family. We have to make sure that we are holding each other accountable for pulling the best out of each other. **If I am truly my brother's keeper, that means I am making sure that he is in the right mind and body at all times.** We are working to push each other to take risks, sacrifice for our families, and put our significant others' needs before our own, all while having a lot of fun.

Being a friend is not all business. Our brothers are also our escape as well. They are the people you turn to when you need a reality check. These are the same dudes you should be able to laugh uncontrollably with and share funny moments, because we grow and develop in those great times as well.

When we venture off on brothers only trips, it helps reconnect to much simpler times. It gives us the opportunity to relax and only think about ourselves. For my married brothers who are reading this book, it is important to allow yourself and your spouse time to travel alone. Marriage and raising children are work. It's great work, but it is work nonetheless. Due to this, it is important that you occasion-

113

ally take a vacation from it all. We must spend time relaxing and laughing away from the work. Developing ourselves means that we have to create the fertile soil and mindset for the growth to happen. The people you keep around you play a vital role in that development.

I've had a great amount of friends within my lifetime...

- Black

All of them served their purpose and helped me grow in some form or fashion. As I look back, I see that my circle of friends was a direct reflection of my mindset at that particular time. I attracted whatever I was and they helped me grow in whatever I was focused on. You can learn a lot about a man by the company he keeps. So insert into my life Mr. Sean Beasy. Beasy was a different type of dude. I mean a super different type of dude. The type of man that I would 'jone' (make jokes about) on in my immature days. Well I still 'jone' on him, so maturation is still happening. I can't really explain Beasy, so I won't try, but what I will say is that he has one of the most purest hearts I've ever encountered. He didn't do too much preaching, however he led by example. He was not swayed by public opinion. If he wanted to do something, he did it regardless of how different it may have appeared to his peers. I respected his character so much. I learned a lot about myself by watching Beasy's moves. Beasy's train of thought challenged my ideas of what I thought manhood was and he also defined what I believe manhood is at this point. He caused me to reflect often, not because he told me to or we had some kind of conversation about it. He made me reflect because I saw what it did for him. By no means do I want to paint Beasy as this perfect being, 'cause Lord knows he had his flaws. However, he committed himself to recognizing his flaws and worked diligently on improving them according to his beliefs. I am who I am because of people like Beasy. He supported and encouraged self-development by being the example.

Remember to tell them the truth.
1.   When they're wrong, they're wrong.
2.   Hold each other accountable for your actions.

In June of 2016, while at an amusement park with my student, I received a call from Black...

-VIC

It's very seldom that I speak with him and he is not happy or dramatic, and today was no different. He started to explain to me the love for his wife and his plan for the marriage. He then concluded that he wanted me to be the best man. I felt honored that he asked me, but I also felt a great sense of responsibility.

As his best man, my job was not just to be there during the days leading up to the wedding, or just on the wedding date. Instead, my duty is to be present for him throughout the marriage, help him remember the vows he took when he walked down the aisle, and help him remember (that during rocky times) there are clearer roads ahead. Imagine if that is how we all approached brotherhood. One of not just service to our brothers, but their families as well. The only way to do that is to hold ourselves accountable for our personal responsibility to the accountability of our best men.

The honesty I discussed a few sections earlier holds true when building a friendship with our brothers. **True friendship can only occur in truth.** We have to have morals and standards in our friendships as well. If you are a friend to someone who is married with children you are just as responsible for your brother's success. Of course a marriage is between two people, but we have the ability to support the building of the union or the dismantling of it. There will be difficult conversations. There will be times when you are going to have to pull each other to the carpet for the mistakes made or offenses done. The conversation may get heated, things may feel uneasy, but these moments are needed if we are to build each other into men that will help sustain generations to come.

About eight years ago, I was asked to host this dope open mic in the DC area...
- Black

Vic's brother, Truth, presented the opportunity to me. His name fits him so well. I never hosted an event before. I was skeptical, but positive, that I would do a good job. He wasn't so sure. How do I know? 'Cause he told me. Lol. This dude is one of the most truthful dudes I've ever met. He says exactly what he feels and he rarely cares if he offends anyone. I grew to love and respect his honesty. Oh, I forgot to mention that Vic was the co-host. I didn't really have a relationship with Vic prior to this show, so I was unsure about our chemistry as co-hosts. He was the well-read "know it all" in my opinion. I was an ignorant, say-anything-to-get-a-laugh type of dude. He was an uplifting, happy Kwanzaa, black-fist type of dude. How the hell is this going to work? Man, it worked perfectly. It was a perfect balance, and people loved the combination.

Fast forward to today. Victorious and Truth are some of my closest friends. The greatest thing about our relationship is that I know I will get honesty from them both. Most of the time, I probably won't like what I hear when it comes to their opinions, because they will probably disagree with me and come with some facts to debunk my opinion. As a human, however, I would prefer that people agreed with me all the time, so that I can be justified in my thoughts or actions. They do not give me that luxury. They challenge everything. I mean everything. Not only do they challenge everything, they also bring it back up in the future and tell me how stupid I was to have ever thought what I thought. I'm not always on the losing side of the debate. They do stupid stuff too, and I challenge them with love. Ultimately, I want the best for them, as I do with all my friends, so I constantly serve them a big bowl of truth.

Become comfortable with restrictions...
- VIC

"No." Say it with me" "Nah, B, I can't do that." There are different variations of how to say "no." There is, "Get the hell 'outta' here with that." And, "Dawg, you lunching, ain't no way I'm doing that." Or there is the classic, "Nope!" In any form you use it, get real comfortable with saying no. If your mind is similar to mine, you are thinking how is saying no being loyal. **It's simple; loyalty in short means that you are staying true.** And that means, that you cannot always do what others need from you. You have to make sure you keep it *100*.

To me, one of the dumbest male contests in the world is when guys try to outdrink their friends...
- Black

What's sad is that people attach being a man to this dumb concept. The more liquor you can drink means that you are more man than someone else. How stupid is that? You mean to tell me that we will rate our manhood on who can drink more poison and get more drunk? And God forbid that you vomit because of the amount of liquor you have drank. Now you a wimp, and you can't hold your liquor. It's even a contest about who can drink alcohol faster. You've heard the term before, "Why you babysitting that drink?" I've never been a big drinker, because I hate not being in control of myself. To me, manhood has a lot to do with being fully aware of what's going on with your surroundings. So why would it be my goal to get so intoxicated that I don't even remember the night before. Nah, I'm good. By no means am I trying to offend people who drink alcohol, because I have my fair share of drinks. To this day, you may catch me with a Long Island Ice Tea in my hand. I'm not holier than thou. However, I know my limitations, and I know when enough is enough for me. This is not just about drinking alcohol. This can be applied to everything in life. Manhood is about knowing your limitations and making sure you don't exceed them regardless of the outside influence. Manhood is about creating restrictions in your life and being comfortable with enforcing them.

CHAPTER XI.

IMPROVE YOUR COMMUNITY

Take chances to change your hood...
- VIC

One of my favorite political organizations was the Black Panther Party for Self Defense founded by Huey Newton and Bobby Seale. What I loved about them the most were the chances they took in changing their hoods. The two things that stood out to me the most was that they had armed patrol men and women who would follow police in their neighborhoods to ensure they were not brutalizing citizens. In addition, they started a free breakfast program for young people before they went to school. Their free breakfast program was seen as one of the biggest threats to the national security of America because they felt like they had the minds of the youth.

The Black Panther Party took chances. Huey Newton had a doctoral degree, but he decided to bring his intelligence back to the hood. Members of the organization carried a copy of the U.S. Constitution in their pockets to ensure they knew the law better than the people enforcing it. They were shining examples of what manhood looks like. **They didn't spend time passing judgements on the conditions, instead they began to take calculated actions to create change.**

As we grow and develop as men, it is important for us to take risks as well. We must begin to figure out ways we can make substantive changes in our neighborhoods and communities. Business as usual is not enough to create the positive change we need. Talking is not enough, we have to begin to think and act in innovative ways to grow, develop and defend our communities.

Your voice matters.

- VIC

I remember when I was young and we would pull up to another man at a traffic light. Folks would mug (frown) at each other and look away. When I was young, I always questioned why we were doing it, but I actively participated every time I pulled up to a red light next to another man. Looking back on it, I understand that it derived from competition. Because we grew up in hardships and tension, we were constantly at odds for resources. Asserting our manhood, even at a traffic light, was a way to feel like men. As we mature, we now understand that to truly assert our manhood, we must be together. **We only become men when our families and communities are thriving.** So instead, when we are at the light now, we throw up a peace sign to signify we are comrades in our struggle to grow our communities.

I was always a big advocate for the youth...
- Black

I've always wanted to do more hands-on work to help our young people, however life's obligations restricted me from going full force. At times, I would beat myself up because I didn't think I was doing enough. To this day, I still think that I am not doing enough and I plan to do more. In 2013, I was unemployed and in need of work. I have a degree and I knew that I could get a corporate job paying good money, but I knew it would take more time than I was willing to give. I also knew that a corporate job probably wouldn't align with my desires to help my community. One day I was talking to Vic and he suggested that I become a substitute teacher at his school. At the time, he was a vice principal of a middle school. He warned me that the money wouldn't be plentiful, however the joy that I would receive from serving would overflow.

I took him up on his offer, but I was never eager to do it. I questioned my ability to reach middle school kids in a classroom setting. I had no problem talking to kids on the street because I could talk to them as if we were homies, but I didn't think this approach would be acceptable in a school setting. Vic assured me that I would do just fine and to just be myself. I've performed in front of 90,000 screaming SOJA fans. I've had songs grace the Billboard list. I've had my music video played on major networks. All of these accomplishments came with a great amount of pride and joy. But nothing, I repeat, nothing compared to the joy that I experienced as a substitute teacher.

See I wasn't your average substitute teacher. I was more like a student advocate. I was more like an adult buddy who had some knowledge to share with young people. I was the teacher that the students could relate to. I was that teacher that never harshly corrected the kids because their pants were sagging, but instead, I lovingly encouraged them to lift up their pants. I would joke with the students. I tried my best to make learning fun for them. In return, they gave me respect and love. They gave me joy. They gave me one of my biggest accomplishments to date, to uplift an entire community. They also let me know that my voice matters. I'm forever indebted to those kids.

Remember, you never really leave your "hood."
1.   Don't look down, unless you are pulling someone up.
2.   Success means nothing unless you are helping someone else become successful.

There are few things I despise more than fake middle-class people who look down on others with tougher financial or environmental struggles...
- VIC

We should be the examples for our communities. There are too many people who pass judgement, without creating long-lasting programs to help others who are less fortunate. Our communities need our actions, not or judgements. **Weak men complain, strong men take action.** Thinking that we are not "role models" is useless and counterproductive. Our good and bad actions are examples for our young people growing up. We are responsible for ensuring the progress of our people.

In schools where I have worked, I often hear adults suggest that students should work hard in school so that they can make money and leave their current neighborhoods. I totally understand the need to live in safe environments, but if all the intelligent people leave, what will be left of the community? Instead we should be instructing our young people to get enough information to come back into their neighborhoods and stimulate positive change. When you find success, please don't disassociate yourself from the neighborhood that raised you. Instead, find ways to actively contribute to it's growth and development.

It's very awkward when someone sees me and freaks out because he/she recognizes me for my accomplishments.

- Black

They proceed to energetically compliment me for whatever accomplishment made them recognize me. This makes me feel so uncomfortable. At these moments, I become speechless. I turn into a robot and just keep saying, "Thank you, thank you so much." I hate my response, because although I'm genuine about my thanks, I say it so much that, to me, it doesn't seem powerful anymore. I would prefer if someone came to me and congratulated me on my accomplishments and then asked about the obstacles I had to overcome to accomplish what I accomplished. This would bring it back home to me. This would give me the opportunity to show how similar our lives are. This would give me the opportunity to encourage them. This would be great for me too, because I don't believe my own hype. I'm just blessed, and I just so happen to be blessed in a field that is attractive to a vast amount of people. We live in a world that pays more attention to the triumph than the journey. Well I'm a story type of dude. I want you to know what it took for me to accomplish what you are currently praising. I want you to know that I come from some of the same environments that you may have. I want you to know that I struggle with self-doubt and fear. I want you to know the good, the bad and the ugly, with hopes that it will encourage you to overcome your obstacles. Yeah, that's manhood for you. Humbling yourself and knowing that you are somehow connected to the next man and it is your duty to build him up as much as possible. That's what manhood is about. I love hip-hop and as dope as hip-hop is, it is such a negative advocate for manhood. There are many things that I can break down in hip-hop that, in my opinion, go against the principles of manhood, but that's another book. I will only focus on one.

The number one issue that comes to mind is when artists receive an amount of money and then separate themselves from the hood. I'm not necessarily talking about location. I don't think it's a smart move to get an abundance of money and live in the hood. You are asking to get robbed. I'm talking about the mental separation. You know, the mental separation that's promoted with phrases like, "Don't talk to me unless you got money."

Really slim? So you're telling me that a broke dude couldn't possibly give you any information that may better your life? Are you also telling me that you refuse to share your knowledge with anyone that is below your pay grade? Wow. True manhood can change this world for the better.

Man-up and embrace a new standard of love, loyalty and leadership. We have a critical opportunity to change our communities, our world, and the future for men coming behind us, but we must first change ourselves and our own mindsets. If you enjoyed this book, make sure you pass it on to another brother, and let's encourage the masses to Man-up.

ABOUT THE AUTHORS

Alfred Duncan is a husband, father emcee and a two-time Grammy-nominated recording artist as the lead vocalist of SOJA Band. He was raised in Prince George's County, Maryland and graduated from Forestville High School where he was president of The Black Male Achievement Group, a perussionist in the award-winning Forestville Marching Band, and played on Forestville's then championship basketball team.

Post-graduation, Alfred attended Shenandoah University in Winchester, Virginia where he played point guard on the men's basketball team and earned a Bachelor of Arts degree in Mass Communications, with a minor in religion. After college, Alfred returned to the Washington, DC area where he held various jobs at companies such as IBM, Dewberry & Davis, and Verizon. He worked as a promotional assistant with WKYS 93.9 FM, where he also created and performed on-air parodies and show introductions.

Now he is known across the United States as "Alfred The MC," the lead vocalist for the band, Mambo Sauce. He is coined one of the most talented lyricists and song writers in the DC area. He wrote the song "Welcome to DC," which is still being played at most Washington, DC professional sports events. Mr. Duncan is also popular amongst Washington Redskins fans for his viral Redskinsthemed remixes played on WPGC 95.5 FM and Comcast SportsNet.

In his spare time, Alfred enjoys giving back to the youth, playing basketball, and spending time with "his boys" – son, Blake, and nephew, Chauncey. He proudly lives by the motto, "work ain't hard", and uses his music and the stage to encourage people everywhere to never stop pursuing their dreams.

Victorious Hall is imperfectly perfect. Made in the image of God, he made plenty of mistakes and has done some good. He was raised in Prince George's County, Maryland with roots in New York. He's African though. Not what how you think, but he is connected to all African people globally. He is connected to the diaspora. He has been a husband for 11 years to a wife that has helped mold the man he is. He has been a father for 9 years. His son King Victorious Jihad has the best of Vic's own soul placed in him. He has worked as an educator all his life: first as a mentor, then a history teacher, and currently a vice-principal. He also travels nationwide to train educators on innovative ways to teach young people. On the weekends and during his down time, Vic enjoys riding his bicycle for hours.

Please leave a review on Amazon.

Visit ForeverDuncan.com/books to order additional books and products.

Connect with Alfred:

@AlfredTheMC on Instagram and Twitter.

Alfred Duncan on Facebook

Connect with Victorious:

@BroVictorious on Instagram and Twitter

Victorious Hall on Facebook

Alfred & Sherrell Duncan's book will be released in 2017. Stay up-to-date with ForeverDuncan.com for all things
#ForeverDuncan.

65341844R00080

Made in the USA
Charleston, SC
16 December 2016